Mickey's Young Readers Library

VOLUME
18
Word Fun
An Activity Book for Young Readers

WRITTEN BY STEVEN OTFINOSKI
EDUCATIONAL CONSULTANT:
THOBURN EDUCATIONAL ENTERPRISES, INC.

A BANTAM BOOK
NEW YORK · TORONTO · LONDON · SYDNEY · AUCKLAND

Word Fun   A Bantam Book/September 1990. All rights reserved.
© 1990 The Walt Disney Company. Developed by The Walt Disney Company in conjunction with Nancy Hall, Inc.
This book may not be reproduced or transmitted in any form or by any means.

ISBN 0-533-05639-5

Published simultaneously in the United States and Canada. Bantam Books are published by Bantam Doubleday
Dell Publishing Group, Inc.
Its trademark, consisting of the words "Bantam Books" and the portrayal of a rooster, is Registered in U.S. Patent
and Trademark Office and in other countries. Marca Registrada. Bantam Books 666 Fifth Avenue, New York, New York 10103.
Printed in the United States of America
0   9   8   7   6   5   4   3   2   1
A Walt Disney BOOK FOR YOUNG READERS

Feline Feelings

Tell how Molly feels in each picture. Match each picture to the feeling word that best describes it. Explain why Molly looks the way she does in each picture.

1.

2.

3.

a. surprised

b. happy

c. sad

Pick A Feeling

Each sentence tells how a character acts when he or she feels a certain way. Say aloud the word that fits best in each sentence. Use the words in the clue box to help you.

angry	sad	happy

1. Molly purrs when she's _____ .

2. Minnie cries when she's _____ .

3. Mickey shakes his finger and speaks loudly when he's _____ .

Mickey's Birthday Scramble

Uncle Scrooge sent Mickey a scrambled birthday message. Help Mickey figure it out by unscrambling the four underlined words.

Dear Mickey,

   Have a <u>paphy</u> birthday! I am <u>das</u> that I can't be there for your party. However, I am <u>lagd</u> that all your other friends will be there.

<u>OVEL</u>,
Uncle Scrooge

Nouns On Grandma's Farm

A *noun* is a word that names a person, place, or thing. Look at the pictures below. Point to the three nouns that name things on Grandma's farm.

pitchfork   bus   haystack   cow

Where might you find the fourth noun?

Grandma Duck's Party

Help Grandma plan a party. Point to the five nouns that name things she will need.

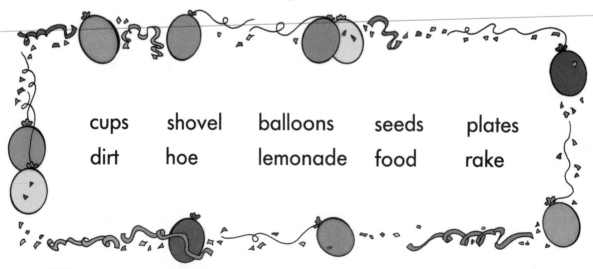

cups   shovel   balloons   seeds   plates

dirt   hoe   lemonade   food   rake

Tell how you might use the things (nouns) she doesn't need for the party.

Nouns And Not Nouns

Help Huey figure out which one of the three words beside each picture is the noun. He's done the first one, but he needs your help to do the rest.

1.   blue, round, (ball)

2.   red, wagon, small

3.   heavy, book, big

4.   oval, brown, football

Which One Doesn't Belong?

Help Elmo find the one thing in each group below
that doesn't belong. Tell why it doesn't belong.

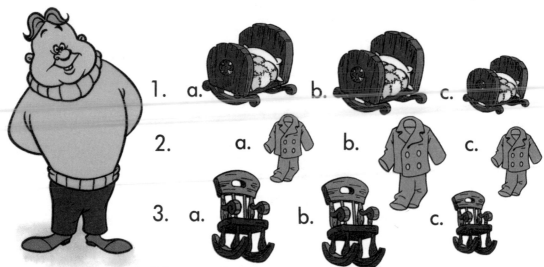

1. a.   b.   c.

2. a.   b.   c.

3. a.   b.   c.

Minnie's Matchup

Help Minnie match each object to the word that best
describes its size. (Hint: Compare all the objects
before you decide which word best describes each thing.)

1.   a. tiny

2.   b. little

3.   c. big

Big, Bigger, Biggest

Look at each set of pictures below and help Minnie answer the questions for each set.

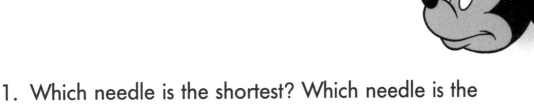

1. Which needle is the shortest? Which needle is the longest?

   a.   b.   c.

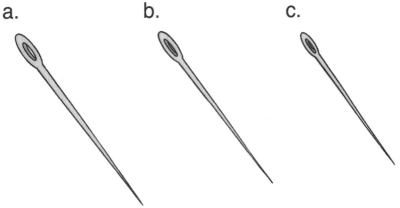

2. Which tree is the tallest? Which tree is the shortest?

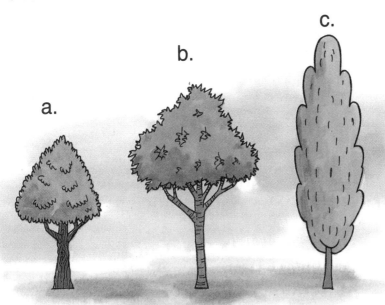

Where Is Pooh?

Look carefully at the pictures of Pooh and answer
the questions.

1. In which picture is Pooh *near*
   his honey pot?

2. In which picture is Pooh *far*
   from his honey pot?

3. In which picture is Pooh at
   the *top* of the tree?

4. In which picture is Pooh at
   the *bottom* of the tree?

5. How many things can you find in your room that
   are *above* you? See how many things are *below*
   you.

Backward Words

Pooh can't believe it, but if you spell the word POOH backward, you get another word. Do you know what the new word is? Help Pooh make new words out of the words below.

1.
TUB spelled backward becomes _____ ?

2.
PAN spelled backward becomes _____ ?

3.
TOP spelled backward becomes _____ ?

How Does The Goose Feel?

An *adjective* is a word that describes or tells you something about a person, place, or thing. Look at the pictures of the goose below. Match each picture with the adjective that best describes the way the goose feels.

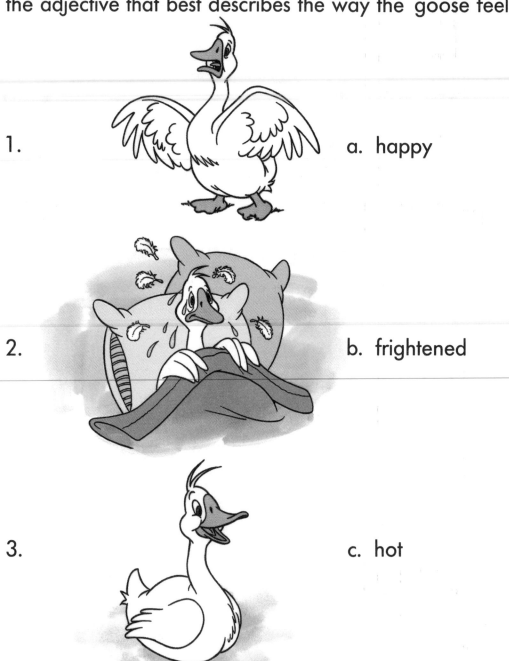

1.

a. happy

2.

b. frightened

3.

c. hot

Golden Egg Hunt

Scrooge is looking for five very special eggs hidden
in this picture. Five of the eggs you will find will
match the *adjectives* (words that describe the eggs) below.

big and golden   rainbow-colored   brown
blue   small and golden

It's All The Same To Me

Synonyms are words that have the same or similar meanings. For example, *happy* and *glad* are synonyms. Look at each labeled picture. Help Goofy name its synonym, using the words in the clue box to help you.

| large | unhappy | little |

Words Of A Genie

This genie can change a word into another by simply adding a *prefix* (a word part that goes before a word to change its meaning). You can be a genie, too. Change each word below by adding the prefix "un" in front of it. How does this change the meaning?

happy	even	stuck	equal	wrap
dress	clear	fair	expected	do

One Thing Is Different!

Help Donald figure out which thing is different in each of the three groups below.

1. a.   b.   c.

2. a.   b.   c.

3. a.   b.   c.

Tool-Time Matchup

Help Donald complete his jobs. Match the job on the left to the correct tool pictured on the right.

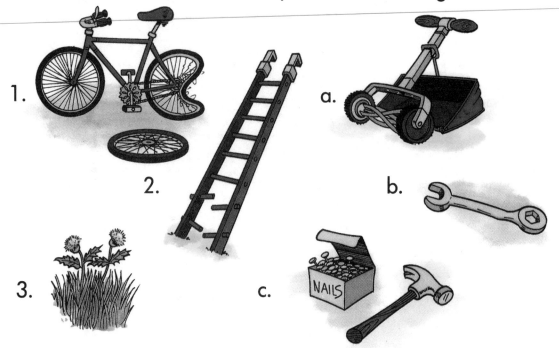

1.

2.

3.

a.

b.

c.

Hidden-Tool Hunt

Help Donald find the seven tools hidden in his messy garage. Point to each tool and name it.

| screwdriver | paintbrush | vise | shears |
| wrench | rake | handsaw | |

What's Going On?

After eating Rabbit's delicious applesauce, Rabbit's guests had lots of fun. Describe what each one is doing.

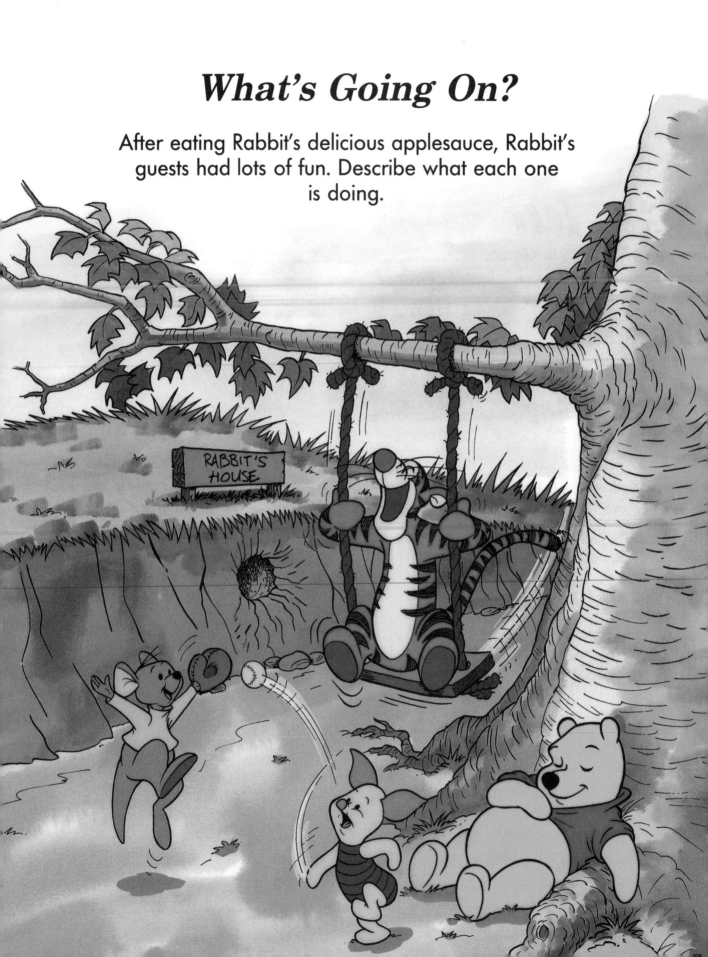

Who's Doing What?

A *verb* is a word that refers to an action. Pooh and his friends are always in action! Match each character with the action word that tells what he is doing.

1.

2.

3.

a. dancing

b. cooking

c. eating

Pooh Says . . .

Pooh would like to play a game with you. He'll name an action, and you act it out! Can you . . .

. . . *bounce* like Tigger?
. . . *run* like Christopher Robin?
. . . *hop* like Roo?
. . . *eat* like Pooh?
. . . *wiggle your nose* like Piglet?

Now act out some of your favorite actions.

Words In A Winter Wonderland

Donald, Goofy, Morty, and Ferdie are playing outside during the big winter storm. How many things that have to do with winter can you find in the picture? Use the clue box below to help you.

snow	sled	skis	snowball	
snowman	mittens	hat	scarf	coat

What To Wear?

Help Goofy figure out which clothes he needs for
winter and which ones he needs for summer. Point to and
name the winter things. Then point to and name the
summer things. Explain why certain things
are better for winter, and why some are better for summer.

Goofy's Simple Recipes

Help Goofy figure out which food doesn't belong in each recipe. Point to the one that doesn't fit.

1. GOOFY'S SUPER SANDWICH SPECIAL
   a. peanut butter   c. bread
   b. jelly   d. pickles

2. GOOFY'S HOUSE SALAD
   a. lettuce   c. ice cream
   b. tomatoes   d. cucumber

Food Word Search

In the word-search puzzle below, help Goofy find the words for the five foods given in the clue box. The words may be found from left to right and top to bottom. Some words share the same letters.

```
C N I D O W P L
A Q U T L P E B
R P I C K L E S
R E S Y U I C Z
O T R A M G H O
T S K H R E E B
S A U S A G E S
E X O M C A S A
G F R U I T E P
```

| cheese | pickles | carrots | fruit | sausages |

All Sorts Of Food

1. Help Donald sort the pictures of food below into the right food groups. Look at the Food-Groups Chart below to help you.

Food-Groups Chart

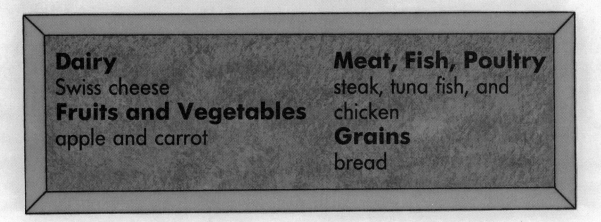

Dairy
Swiss cheese
Fruits and Vegetables
apple and carrot

Meat, Fish, Poultry
steak, tuna fish, and chicken
Grains
bread

milk

cereal

orange

turkey

broccoli

2. Can you think of more foods for each group?

First Things First

Can you figure out the first letter in each animal pictured below? Say aloud the name of each animal. 1. What is its first letter? 2. How many other things do you know that begin with the same first letter?

Odd Letter Out

Find the one thing that doesn't begin with the same letter as the others in each of the groups below.

1. a.   b.   c.

2. a.   b.   c.

3. a.   b.   c.

Letter Hunt

Before the witch returns, find something that begins with the letter *d.* Find something that begins with the letter *l.*
Find something that begins with the letter *h.*

Things That Go

Below are four things that go from place
to place. They carry people and
things. Can you name them?

1.

2.

3.

4.

Which thing goes in the air?
Which thing goes in the water?
Which things go on the ground?

Things That Go And Things That Don't

Which two things pictured below can go from place to place? Now point to the ones that can't.

plant   dog   wagon   tree

1.

2.

3.

4.

What is different about the way the two things that go move?

Bicycle Matchup

Help Mickey match the words below to the bicycle parts they name. Point to the part in the picture and tell what it does.

handlebars   spokes   tires   handbrakes   pedals

A Sign For Mickey's Shop

Get a piece of paper and some crayons or markers. Help Mickey make a sign for his bike shop. A good sign should have the following details:

The shop's name

The kind of work done there

Days and hours
the shop is open

Special services
to attract customers

Draw your sign on another sheet of paper.

Mickey's Tricky Riddle

Here's a bicycle riddle that Mickey told to Morty and Ferdie. Read it carefully and tell how many were going to St. Roy's. (Hint: The picture contains a clue to the answer.)

As I was going to St. Roy's,
I met a man with seven boys,
Every boy had seven bikes,
Every bike had seven wheels,
Every wheel had seven spokes,
Spokes, wheels, bikes, boys,
How many were going to St. Roy's?

Sounding Off!

Goofy's car, *Old Faithful,* makes many different sounds. How many sounds listed below can you make?

Say the words aloud. Do you think any of these words sound like their sounds? Can you think of some other words that describe sounds?

Match A Sound

Each thing pictured below has a sound all its own.
Match each sound word to the object that
makes that sound.

1.   pop   a.

2.   tick tock   b.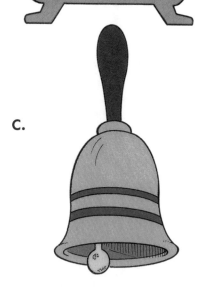

3.   ding dong   c.

Silly Words

A *palindrome* is a word that is the same whether it is spelled backward or forward.

1. Which of the words below are palindromes?
2. Can you think of any others?

DAD MOM POP BOB GUS
SIS TOOT PIG PEEP

Rhyme Time

Help Scrooge think of words that rhyme with the word "silly." (Hint: Try replacing the "s" in silly with every letter of the alphabet.)

A Silly Limerick

A *limerick* is a silly rhyme. Read the limerick about Scrooge and his money. Then say the words that complete the poem. Use the clue box for help. (Hint: lines 1, 2, and 5 should rhyme with each other, and lines 3 and 4 should rhyme with each other.)

1. There once was a duck who was funny,
2. And worried all day about _____ .
3. Then Donald and Daisy
4. Told Scrooge he was _____ .
5. In Duckburg since then, life's been _____ .

| sunny | money | crazy |

Mixed-Up Rainbow

That tricky troll is at it again! He's mislabeled all the colors in the rainbow. Tell Mickey which color words belong on which bands of color.

red
yellow
purple
orange
green
blue

Color-Word Jumble

Help Mickey unscramble the five color words below.
Then match each color word to its proper crayon.

1.

2.

3.

4.

5.

a. NPKI

b. ERUPPL

c. HTIWE

d. KLACB

e. RNOWB

Place That Woodchuck!

Figure out each Woodchuck's place in line from left to right.

1. Who is the third Woodchuck?
2. Who is the fifth?
3. Who is the eighth?

Trophy Trouble

Help Donald match the right T-shirts to the right trophies.

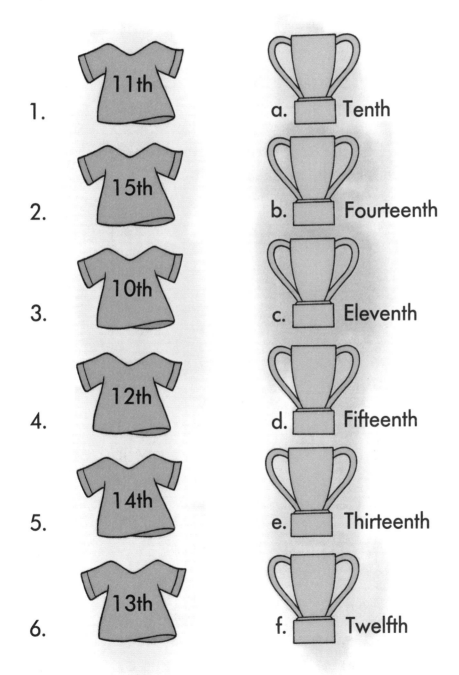

1. 11th

a. Tenth

2. 15th

b. Fourteenth

3. 10th

c. Eleventh

4. 12th

d. Fifteenth

5. 14th

e. Thirteenth

6. 13th

f. Twelfth

ANSWERS

Feline Feelings *(page 6)*
1. b   2. c   3. a

Pick A Feeling *(page 6)*
1. happy   2. sad   3. angry

Mickey's Birthday Scramble *(page 7)*
happy; sad; glad; love

Nouns On Grandma's Farm *(page 8)*
pitchfork; haystack; cow
You would find a bus on a road.

Grandma Duck's Party *(page 8)*
The following items may be used for the party:
cups, balloons, plates, lemonade, food.
Answers may vary.

Nouns And Not Nouns *(page 9)*
1. ball   2. wagon   3. book   4. football

Which One Doesn't Belong? *(page 10)*
1. c This cradle is small, the others are large.
2. b This suit is large, the others are small.
3. c This chair is small, the others are large.

Minnie's Matchup *(page 10)*
1. c   2. b   3. a

Big, Bigger, Biggest *(page 11)*
1. The shortest needle is c. The longest needle is a.
2. The tallest tree is c. The shortest tree is a.

Where Is Pooh? (page 12)

1. a   2. b   3. c   4. d
5. Answers may vary.

Backward Words (page 13)

POOH spelled backward becomes HOOP.
1. TUB spelled backward becomes BUT.
2. PAN spelled backward becomes NAP.
3. TOP spelled backward becomes POT.

How Does The Goose Feel? (page 14)

1. b   2. c   3. a

Golden Egg Hunt (page 15)

It's All The Same To Me (page 16)

small/little; big/large; sad/unhappy

Words Of A Genie (page 17)

unhappy; uneven; unstuck; unequal; unwrap;
undress; unclear; unfair; unexpected; undo. In
each case, when you add the prefix "un" the new
word is the opposite of the original word.

One Thing Is Different! (page 18)

1. b   2. c   3. b

Tool-Time Matchup *(page 18)*
1. b   2. c   3. a

Hidden-Tool Hunt *(page 19)*

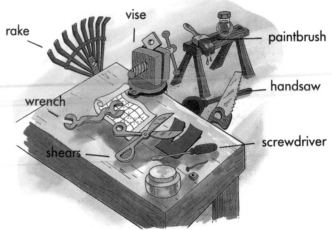

rake

vise

paintbrush

handsaw

wrench

screwdriver

shears

What's Going On? *(page 20)*
Tigger is swinging. Pooh is sleeping.
Piglet and Roo are playing ball.

Who's Doing What? *(page 21)*
1. b   2. a   3. c

Pooh Says . . . *(page 21)*
Answers may vary.

Words In A Winter Wonderland *(page 22)*

hat

mittens

snowman

scarf

coat

snow

sled

snowball   skis

What To Wear? (page 23)
The winter clothes: earmuffs, scarf, mittens, coat, snowshoes.
The summer clothes: shorts, summer shirt.
Heavier clothes are better for winter to keep your body warm.
Lighter clothes are better for summer to keep your body cool.
Answers may vary slightly.

Goofy's Simple Recipes (page 24)
1. d   2. c

Food Word Search (page 24)

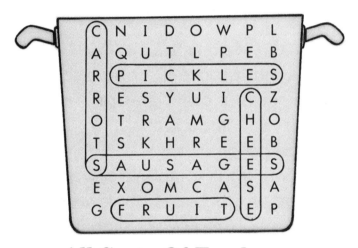

All Sorts Of Food (page 25)
1. The orange and broccoli belong to the Fruits and
Vegetables group. The milk belongs to the Dairy group.
The turkey belongs to the Meat, Fish, and Poultry group.
The cereal belongs to the Grains group.
2. Answers may vary.

First Things First (page 26)
1. Horse begins with *h*. Bird begins with *b*.
Dog begins with *d*.
2. Answers may vary.

Odd Letter Out (page 26)
1. b   2. b   3. c

Letter Hunt (page 27)
d: dog.   l: lemon.   h: horse.

Things That Go (page 28)
1. roller skates   2. bus
3. airplane   4. boat

The airplane goes in the air.
The boat goes in the water.
The bus and the roller skates go on the ground.

Things That Go And Things That Don't (page 29)
The two things that go are the dog and the wagon.
The two things that don't go are the tree and
the plant.
The dog can go on its own, using its legs. The
wagon can only go if someone pushes or pulls it,
and the wagon goes on its wheels.
Answers may vary slightly.

Bicycle Matchup (page 30)

handlebars
handbrakes
spokes
pedals
tires

Discuss with your child how bicycle parts work.
Answers may vary.

A Sign For Mickey's Shop (page 30)
Answers may vary.

Mickey's Tricky Riddle *(page 31)*

Only one person, Mickey, was going to St. Roy's. Everyone else was headed in the other direction, away from St. Roy's.

Sounding Off! *(page 32)*

Answers may vary.

Match A Sound *(page 33)*

1. b   2. a   3. c

Silly Words *(page 34)*

1. The palindromes are: WOW; MOM; POP; BOB; DAD; SIS; TOOT; PEEP.

2. Answers may vary.

Rhyme Time *(page 34)*

Some words that rhyme with silly are: Billy, dilly, filly, hilly, Millie, Tillie, Willie.

A Silly Limerick *(page 35)*

2. money   4. crazy   5. sunny

Mixed-Up Rainbow *(page 36)*

The correct order of colors from bottom to top is: red, orange, yellow, green, blue, purple.

Color-Word Jumble *(page 37)*

1. c   2. e   3. a
4. d   5. b

Place That Woodchuck! *(page 38)*

1. Huey   2. Dewey   3. Louie

Trophy Trouble *(page 39)*

1. c   2. d   3. a
4. f   5. b   6. e

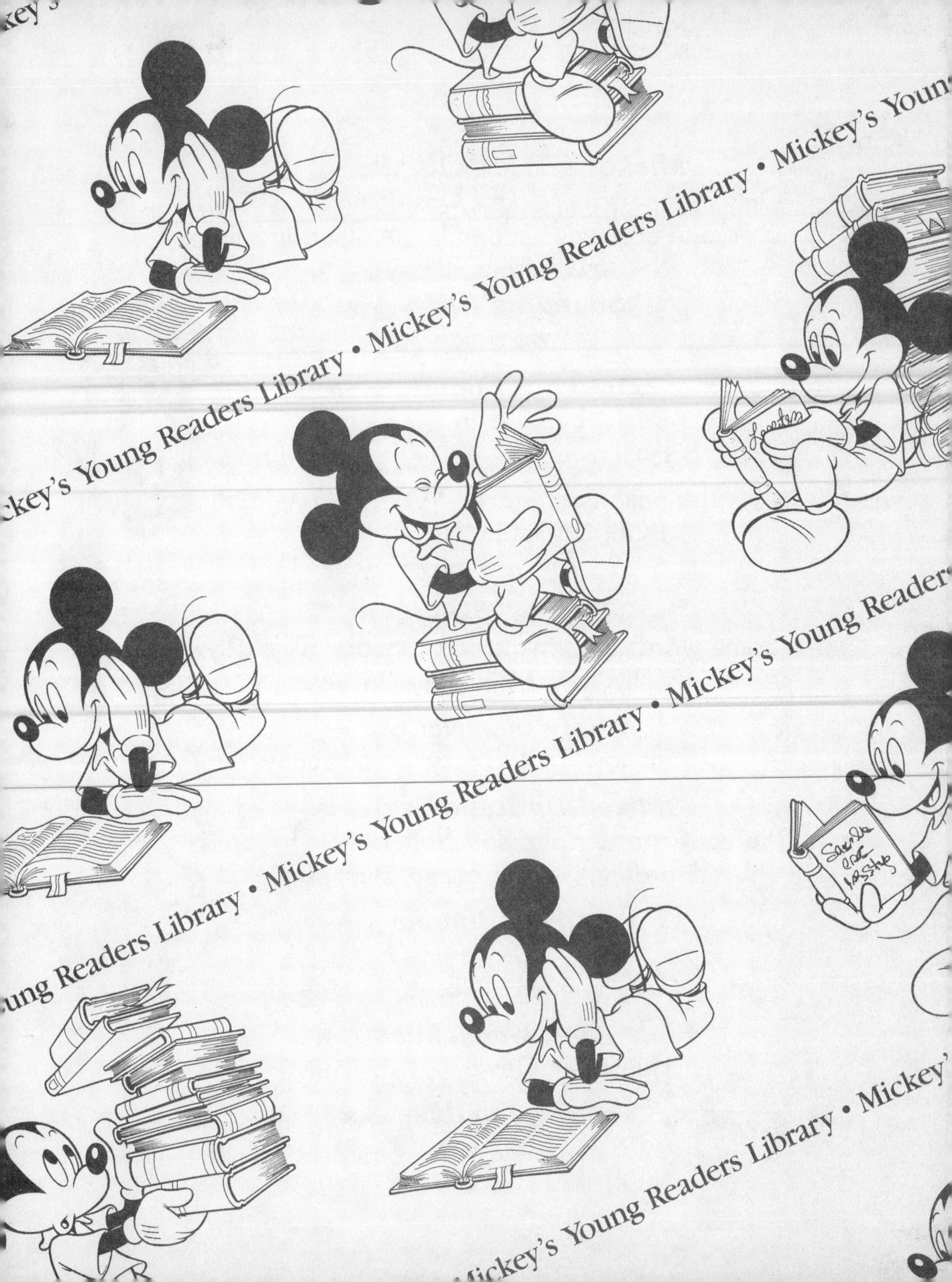